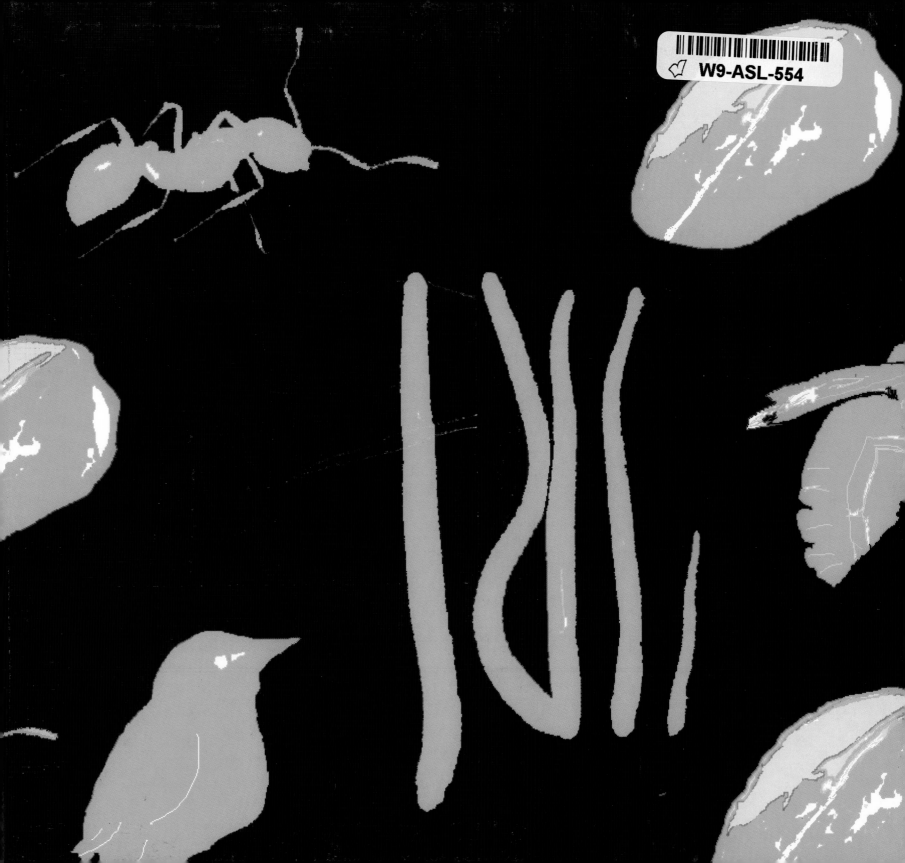

Exotic Invaders

Killer Bees, Fire Ants, and Other Alien Species Are Infesting America!

Jeanne M. Lesinski

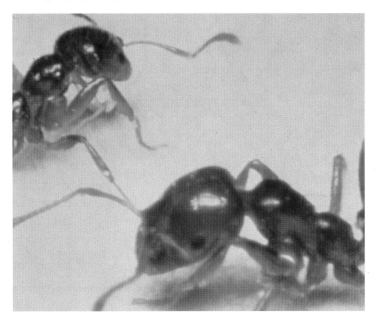

Walker and Company
New York

To my family, near and far

First published in the United States of America in 1996 by Walker Publishing Company, Inc.

Published simultaneously in Canada by Thomas Allen & Son Canada, Limited, Markham, Ontario

Library of Congress Cataloging-in-Publication Data
Lesinski, Jeanne M.
Exotic invaders : killer bees, fire ants, and other alien species are infesting America! / Jeanne M. Lesinski
p. cm.
Includes bibliographical references (p. 48) and index.
Summary: Describes five species that are not native to North America—the sea lamprey, fire ants, zebra mussels, European starlings, and African honeybees—and efforts to handle the problems their introduction has caused.
ISBN 0-8027-8390-2 (hardcover). — ISBN 0-8027-8391-0 (reinforced)
1. Nonindigenous pests—United States—Juvenile literature. 2. Nonindigenous pests—Control—United States—Juvenile literature. 3. Pest introduction—United States—Juvenile literature. [1. Pests. 2. Animal introduction.] I. Title.
SB990.5.U6L47   1996
591.6′5′0973—dc20   95-20908
CIP
AC

Photograph on title page by Bastiaan M. Drees, courtesy of the Texas Agricultural Extension Service; photograph on copyright page by C. Ramcharan, courtesy of Wisconsin Sea Grant; photograph on contents page provided by James R. Page.

Book design by Janice Noto-Helmers

Printed in Hong Kong

10 9 8 7 6 5 4 3 2 1

Contents

Introduction

Since the European discovery of North America, more than 4,500 exotic species—plants, animals, and microbes found beyond their natural ranges—have established free-living populations in the United States. Today we take many non-native species for granted, like wheat, soybeans, and cattle. Early immigrants, homesick for Europe, imported house sparrows for pets, and biologists introduced the ring-necked pheasant and brown trout for sport.

Few invaders have entered the United States on their own. Instead they have been introduced either purposefully or accidentally. Some have been transported by unknowing travelers, as contaminants of cargo, in packing materials and shipping containers, or in ships' ballast. Others were intentionally

Sea lampreys are ancient fish, well adapted to their role as predator. (Gregg Baldwin, U.S. Fish and Wildlife Service)

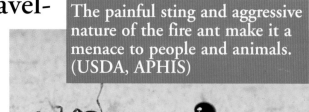

The painful sting and aggressive nature of the fire ant make it a menace to people and animals. (USDA, APHIS)

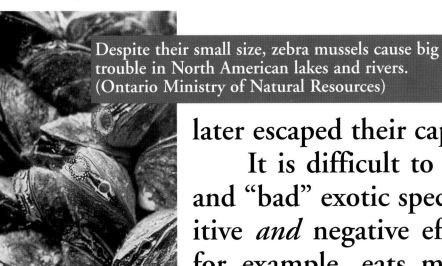

Despite their small size, zebra mussels cause big trouble in North American lakes and rivers. (Ontario Ministry of Natural Resources)

imported as pets or for scientific experiments and later escaped their captors.

It is difficult to distinguish between a "good" and "bad" exotic species for many exotics have positive *and* negative effects. The European starling, for example, eats many insect pests, but it also devours crops. Sadly, many invaders drive out native species or destroy their habitat. Almost every part of the United States battles at least one major pest invader, at an annual cost of billions of dollars nationwide.

Exotic Invaders tells the story of five exotic species: the sea lamprey and zebra mussel that infest lakes and streams, the African honeybee and fire ant that threaten the southern states, and the well-known European starling, whose great energy and adaptability remind us of ourselves.

The starling is a pest to many, plaguing farmers and city dwellers alike. (James R. Page)

The African honeybee is a hardy pioneer from the South. No one knows how far north it can survive. (Charles Cole)

5

The lamprey uses its amazing mouth for more than just feeding. When swimming upstream in a fast current, it sucks on stones and creeps along them so it doesn't get swept away. The lamprey also sucks on stones to drag them from place to place. For these habits, scientists call the species *Petromyzon marinus,* which means "sucker of stone that lives in the sea." (Great Lakes Exotic Species Graphic Library)

During its lifetime, a single lamprey eats forty pounds (eighteen kilograms) of fish. (U.S. Fish and Wildlife Service)

Charter boat captain Larry Watts knows that sportfishing is uncertain business in the Great Lakes. If his client is lucky, a twenty-pound lake trout strikes the lure and puts up a fight for some twenty minutes. Yet all too often, as Watts and his client hoist the trout into the net, they find a hungry lamprey clinging to the fish's silvery side. Watts knows from the disgusted look on his client's face that the fish is no trophy—it was a lamprey's lunch.

Vampire Fish: Sea Lampreys

The sea lamprey is a slender, tube-shaped fish with a mouth like a suction cup. Inside are rows of hard, hooked teeth and a tongue with more teeth on it. The sea lamprey uses its toothy suction-cup mouth to feed on other fish: It swims alongside a large fish and latches on to it with its mouth. Then, using its teeth and tongue, it files a hole in the fish and drinks the fish's blood and other body fluids, only letting go when it is no longer hungry or when the fish dies.

The sea lamprey is one of nine species of lampreys that live in oceans, rivers, and streams in the Northern Hemisphere. In the early 1900s, sea lampreys that lived in the St. Lawrence River, Lake Champlain, and Lake Ontario traveled through the

Erie Canal and invaded the Finger Lakes in New York. Hitching rides on boat hulls, the lampreys quickly spread through the newly opened Welland Ship Canal between Lake Ontario and Lake Erie and then invaded the other Great Lakes: Erie, Huron, Michigan, and Superior. These landlocked lampreys changed the Great Lakes forever.

The Menu
(in order of preference)

lake trout	lake whitefish
chub	white sucker
redhorse	longnose sucker
yellow perch	rainbow trout
burbot	channel catfish
walleye	northern pike
carp	

To satisfy their large appetites, the lampreys killed hundreds of thousands of fish. Because there was so much food for the lampreys, they were able to reproduce in great numbers. By the mid-1950s, sportfishing was nearly ruined, and most owners of fishing boats had gone out of business.

Each year in late winter, adult lampreys crowd around the mouths of rivers and swim upstream in search of nest sites. Together a male and female build a nest of stones on the streambed, and in mid-June, when the water warms, they mate. The female releases twenty to forty eggs at a time, while the male releases milt, a sperm-bearing fluid that fertilizes them. Over several days, the female lamprey may lay as many as 110,000 eggs altogether. These sticky eggs hold to the sand and spaces between the stones of the nest. Exhausted by these efforts, the adult lampreys die within days.

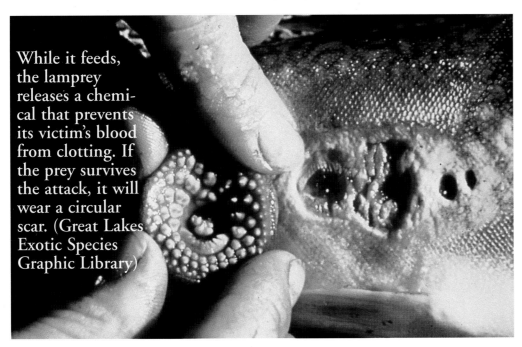

While it feeds, the lamprey releases a chemical that prevents its victim's blood from clotting. If the prey survives the attack, it will wear a circular scar. (Great Lakes Exotic Species Graphic Library)

About one of every hundred eggs hatches into a young lamprey, called an ammocoete. About one-quarter inch (.6 centimeters) long and as thin as a needle, the ammocoete floats downstream into pools with sand or mud bottoms. Tail first, it digs into the mud and, unless washed away by erosion, lives in the burrow from four to seven years. As many as seventeen ammocoetes may live in one square foot of stream bottom. To eat, the ammocoetes simply poke their heads out of their burrows and feed on small

Free swimming parasitic phase in lake; death of adults

1-1½ years

emergence

migration (winter)

migration (spring)

3-14 years

Sedentary larval phase in streams

The lamprey preys on fish only during the last stage of its life. (C. Gill, Great Lakes Basin Commission)

Lamprey Enemies

Two types of minnows eat fresh lamprey eggs, and many animals eat ammocoetes, including water snakes, raccoons, muskrats, minks, weasels, and foxes. Some kinds of gulls, herons, hawks, owls, and bitterns find these young lampreys to be a tasty meal, too. Other fish, such as northern pike, walleye, and brown trout, eat ammocoetes as well. In Europe, people trade recipes for lamprey dishes.

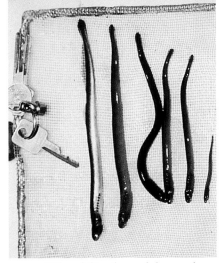

The blind and harmless ammocoete changes into a hungry predator. (U.S. Fish and Wildlife Service)

water plants and animals.

During its life in the burrow, the ammocoete grows from needle size to pencil size. What happens next is quite dramatic. Within three months, while still in the burrow, it grows large, bulging eyes, a sucking disk full of teeth, a filelike tongue, and large fins. Its back becomes blue gray and its belly white.

Now the lamprey floats downstream to open water. It is ready to feast on fish. The lamprey has very keen eyesight and is a

Since the late 1940s, North American fishery biologists have been collecting and carefully studying the lamprey. (Great Lakes Exotic Species Graphic Library)

powerful swimmer. Its prey does not realize that it is in danger until it is too late. After the lamprey latches on to its prey, the fish thrashes wildly, but it cannot break the suction of the lamprey's mouth. A lamprey may feed on a large fish for days before its victim dies.

In the battle to control the sea lamprey, fishery biologists use several weapons: barriers, chemicals, and other lampreys. At river mouths biologists have built short, V-shaped dams called weirs to prevent lampreys from going upriver to spawn. While some weirs are just low

The lamprey barrier must be steep enough to prevent lampreys from sucking on it and inching themselves to the top—and over. (Canadian Department of Fisheries and Oceans)

How You Can Help

1. Do not use live young lampreys as bait for fishing. It is illegal to do so because the lampreys may escape and spread to new areas.
2. If you see lampreys spawning in a stream, report this information to a natural resource manager. You may have discovered a new spawning area.
3. Do not move lampreys over barriers in streams.
4. If your catch was a lamprey's dinner, report this to a biologist at the Great Lakes Fishery Commission, 2100 Commonwealth Boulevard, Suite 209, Ann Arbor, MI 48105-1563.

dams, others use electricity—like an electric fence—to keep out lampreys. Unfortunately, these weirs also block other fish that can't jump, are expensive, and often don't block enough water during spring floods when lampreys spawn.

Because weirs can't eliminate lampreys already living in river bottoms, researchers looked for a chemical that would kill ammocoetes. They tested more than six thousand chemicals before they discovered TFM (3-trifluoromethyl-4-nitrophenol) in 1957. This chemical kills lampreys without harming humans, other mammals, waterfowl, or water plants. Yet too much TFM will kill some sportfish (walleye and northern pike) and aquatic insects, so fishery biologists take special care when they use it.

In 1992, biologists began using a new process. Each year they catch thousands of adult male lampreys that are ready to spawn. They sterilize them with a chemical and return them to streams. These males mate with female lampreys, but their eggs do not mature.

Biologists carefully apply TFM to streams to kill ammocoetes. (Minnesota Sea Grant)

After many years of hard work and hundreds of millions of dollars spent, far fewer lampreys swim the Great Lakes today than thirty years ago—only about one for every ten. Still, these vampire fish kill hundreds of thousands of fish each year, and scientists continue to search for new weapons in their battle to control them.

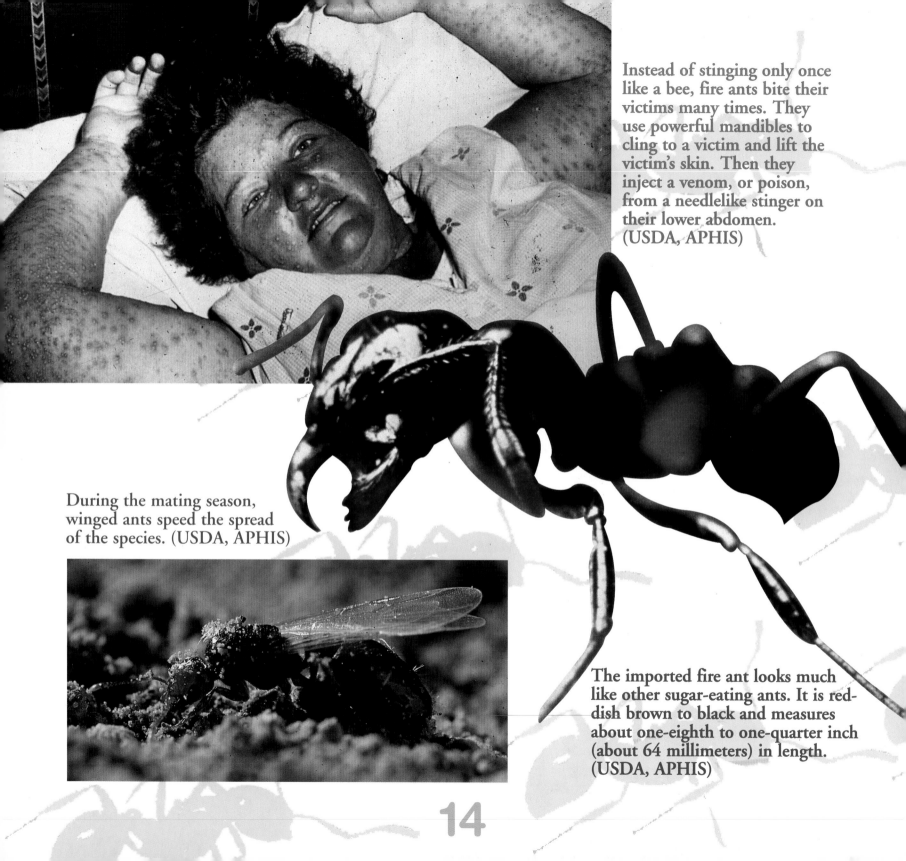

Instead of stinging only once like a bee, fire ants bite their victims many times. They use powerful mandibles to cling to a victim and lift the victim's skin. Then they inject a venom, or poison, from a needlelike stinger on their lower abdomen. (USDA, APHIS)

During the mating season, winged ants speed the spread of the species. (USDA, APHIS)

The imported fire ant looks much like other sugar-eating ants. It is reddish brown to black and measures about one-eighth to one-quarter inch (about 64 millimeters) in length. (USDA, APHIS)

On April 2, 1994, an elderly woman lay in the first-floor Intensive Care Unit at a hospital in West Palm Beach, Florida. She had undergone surgery and was resting. Suddenly she felt a wave of stinging little bites over her body and she pressed her call button to summon the nurses. The nurses told her the surgery caused the strange tingling feeling, but they were wrong. When she looked under her covers, she saw that a swarm of fire ants was crawling over her body. Nurses rushed her screaming from the room and sealed it, and then treated the woman's fire ant bites—more than one hundred of them.

Wildfire: Imported Fire Ants

The red imported fire ant earned its name from its aggressive "fiery" nature and the painful, burning sensation of its stings. Its scientific name, *Solenopsis invicta,* means unbeatable.

Fire ants originally came from Brazil. Sometime in the 1930s they arrived in Alabama, in the dry ballast of ships from South America. The ants spread like wildfire throughout many of the southern and central states.

During the mating season fire ants have wings and may fly up to a mile from their original nest. They also travel as passengers on cars, trucks, trains, or soil-moving equipment, such as bulldozers. Ants often ride in shipments of nursery stock (plants with soil attached to their roots), soil, hay, wood, gravel, and sod. Entomologists, scientists who study insects, predict that fire ants will someday reach as far as California by traveling along the southern part of the United States.

The fire ant lives up to its name. When it stings, its victim feels a burning sensation, like getting burned by a match. Fire ants can swarm over people and their pets, biting them repeatedly when they encounter them in yards, parks, and fields. They are especially dangerous to small children and older people, who may have trouble getting away from the attacking ants. Most of the more than three mil-

The Menu

grease
insects
meat
plants
sugary substances

Imported Fire Ant
Range Map

lion Americans stung by fire ants each year are children. If a person is allergic to ant bites, he or she may become very ill and die. Even when a person is not allergic, the bites are extremely painful and itch for days.

Particularly during dry, hot months, fire ants search for food and moisture in buildings. Sometimes a whole colony of ants will nest in rafters or empty places between walls. Like many ants, fire ants cannot resist electricity. They often gather around electrical switches, air conditioners, utility boxes, and airport runway lights. They move soil into these places and chew on soft materials, like insulation, causing power outages and fires. When the ants short-circuit traffic lights, they cause traffic jams. Researchers do not know why these ants are attracted to electricity, but they do know that electrocuted ants give off a scent (called a pheromone) that attracts other ants to the site.

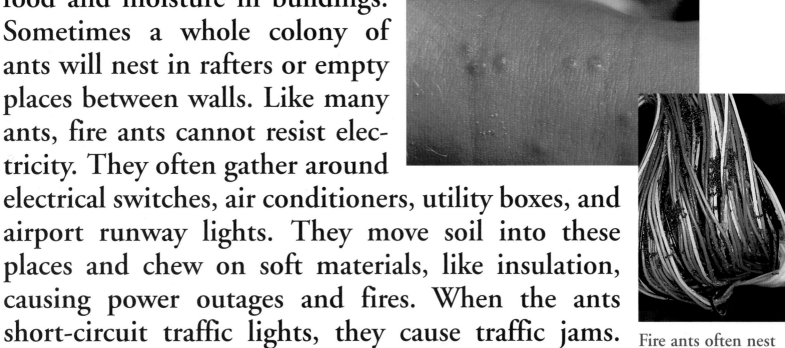

Fire ant venom causes the area around the bite to swell and a small white blister to bubble up. This painful pustule often becomes infected. (S. B. Vinson, Texas Agricultural Extension Service)

Fire ants often nest near or in electrical units, causing breakdowns when they chew through electrical insulation. (S. B. Vinson, Texas Agricultural Extension Service)

Farmers have mixed feelings about fire ants. Though the ants prey on certain pests—pecan weevils, hickory shuckworms, cotton boll weevils, and sugarcane borers—they devour corn and sorghum seeds and seedlings.

In their home country, Brazil, fifty creatures and even some types of fungi kill fire ants, controlling their numbers. In the United States, however, only a few enemies prey on fire ants and these predators cannot control fire ants by themselves.

In 1957, the United States Department of Agriculture (USDA) declared war on the fire ant. The

Fire ants can stunt the growth of or kill the plants they eat, such as watermelon, cucumber, and sunflower seedlings, and mature peanut, soybean, and, as shown here, okra plants. (S. B. Vinson, Texas Agricultural Extension Service)

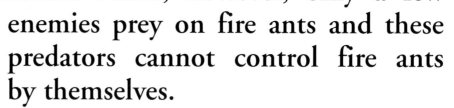

Dozens of queens and as many as several hundred winged ants live in a colony. Worker ants number from 100,000 to 500,000. (USDA, APHIS)

18

Animal and Plant Health Inspection Service (APHIS) established quarantines in the southern states, and these quarantines are still in effect today. Agricultural inspectors examine plants and other items, like hay bales, before they can be moved out of the quarantined area.

Since fire ants arrived in the United States, people have used many different pesticides to kill them. Some of these chemicals caused nasty surprises. In the late 1950s, scientists discovered that one of the pesticides used to kill fire ants—Mirex—also killed many other creatures: helpful insects, fish, frogs, birds, and mammals. Doctors also suspected that Mirex could cause cancer in humans. In 1971, after learning of the dangers, the Environmental Protection Agency (EPA) banned the use of Mirex.

Colonies of fire ants inhabit mushroom-shaped mounds located in sunny, open places. An abundance of large ant mounds can make it impossible to plow or harvest fields. Animals grazing in such fields get stung and can sometimes die from the venom. (USDA, APHIS)

How You Can Help

1. If there is a quarantine in your area, obey the law. Do not move items, such as hay, wood, soil, sod, and gravel, to other areas until they have been inspected for fire ants.

2. Wear protective clothing while outside. Wear shoes or boots, and tuck pant legs into socks.

3. If stung, wash the bite carefully. Use a local antihistamine/painkiller, like Benadryl or Cortisone, to deaden the pain and reduce itching.

4. If you are allergic to ant bites keep a doctor-prescribed epinephrine pen handy. You may want to ask an allergy specialist if desensitization is right for you.

5. Discourage ants from looking indoors for food by keeping your kitchen clean, as well as any other area where food is stored or eaten.

6. Use only small amounts of pesticides such as Award, Amdro, or Ascend.

7. Try not to kill ants that compete with fire ants for food and living space.

8. Do not drown ant mounds with boiling water, gasoline, bleach, acid, or ammonia or use special ant-killing heaters, explosives, or sound makers.

9. For more information, contact the United States Department of Agriculture, Animal and Plant Health Inspection Service, Washington, DC 20250 or your local Cooperative Extension agent listed under the U.S. government heading in your telephone book.

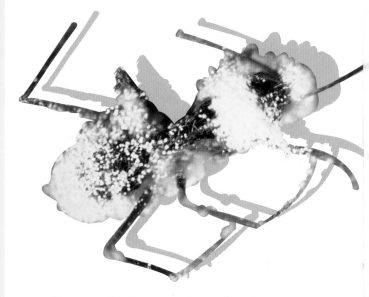

Entomologists work to develop nonchemical control methods, like this ant-eating fungus. (Roberto Pereina)

The safer pesticides now sold are only part of the answer to the fire ant invasion. More fire ants than ever now live in many areas that were sprayed in the 1950s and 1960s. This may be so because the pesticides killed insects and other animals that eat ants or that compete with them for food and nest sites.

To lower the amount of any pesticides used, entomologists search for new ways to control fire ants. Some entomologists made a hormone called Pro-Drone that stops ant larvae from growing into adults. Others are testing fire ant predators from South America: parasitic flies and ants, and even an ant-eating fungus. Entomologists hope to bring some of these ant killers to the United States someday. In the meantime, we need to protect ourselves from imported fire ants and work to keep them from moving into new areas. But we may find that fire ants live up to their scientific name: They may be unbeatable.

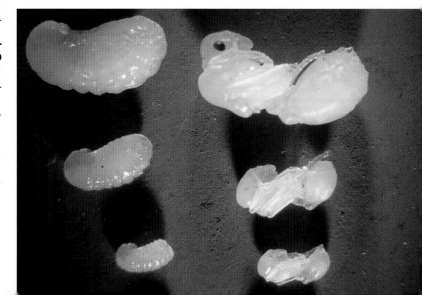

Like many insects, ants undergo metamorphosis. Larvae, small wormlike creatures, hatch from eggs and turn into pupae ten days later. After a week or two they emerge as adults. Scientists are testing hormones that will stop ant larvae from maturing. (S. B. Vinson, Texas Agricultural Extension Service)

Not all zebra mussels look alike. They vary slightly in size and color. (E. Marsden)

Blasting zebra mussels from Detroit Edison's water intake pipes is a costly chore. (Detroit Edison)

On December 15, 1989, workers at the Monroe Water Department in southern Michigan realized they were in trouble. For some mysterious reason water pressure at the plant was dropping. The emergency water shortage shut down schools, businesses, and restaurants. Doctors at the Mercy Memorial Hospital canceled surgeries and sent patients home. Water department workers soon discovered that a combination of ice crystals and millions of zebra mussels had blocked the pipes the waterworks used to draw water from Lake Erie. While workers set up pumps to draw water from a nearby river, fifty-five thousand residents had to use bottled water.

Mighty Mouths: Zebra Mussels

The scientific name for these invaders is *Dreissena polymorpha,* but people call them zebra mussels because of their dark and light brown stripes. Zebra mussels are new to North America, and like many immigrants, they came by boat. Biologists think that in 1986 they hitchhiked across the Atlantic Ocean in the ballast tanks of ships from the Caspian Sea, a freshwater sea in southern Russia.

Some of these freighters traveled by way of the St. Lawrence Seaway to the Great Lakes. When the ships blew out their ballast water in Lake St. Clair, near Detroit, they loosed millions of young zebra mussels, which floated on water currents.

Zebra Mussel Range Map

Newly spawned mussels, microscopic in size, traveled in the water trapped on bird feathers or animal fur, and adult zebra mussels rode on the hulls of boats. After a few years, zebra mussels were running wild in all five Great Lakes and in nearby rivers and smaller lakes.

Where there is one zebra mussel, there will soon be a crowd. Every year, one adult zebra mussel can produce thirty thousand more mussels. When first spawned, zebra mussels are

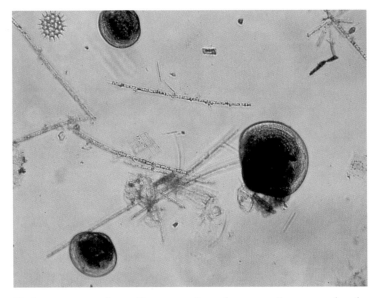

Zebra mussel veligers, already starting to look like clams, are at the mercy of water currents until they sink and attach to a hard surface. (C. Ramcharan, Wisconsin Sea Grant)

called veligers and are so small that twelve thousand could sit on a pencil eraser. At this age they float wherever the water currents take them. They grow quickly as they gobble up tiny water plants and animals called plankton. When about two weeks old, they sink to the bottom and attempt to glue themselves to a firm surface. Nine out of every ten veligers do not land on a firm surface and die. But within three weeks, the surviving veligers already look like tiny clams.

Zebra mussels are very hardy pioneers. They can live out of the water for fourteen days if the air is moist. They can survive hot temperatures of one hundred degrees Fahrenheit (thirty-eight degrees Centigrade). They can even live without food for a year.

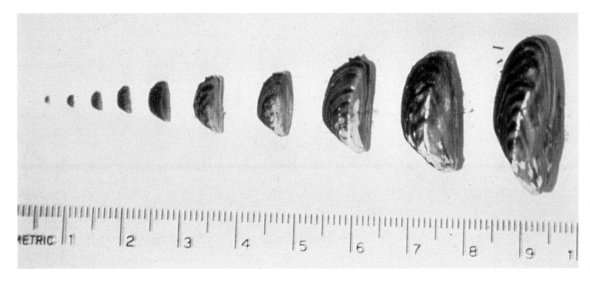

During its first year, a zebra mussel can grow up to one and one-half inches (four centimeters) long, the average size for an adult zebra mussel. (C. Ramcharan, Wisconsin Sea Grant)

A zebra mussel usually lives from three to five years. Large beds of mussels may die all at once. When this happens, the rotting mussels pollute the water, and their sharp shells wash up on beaches.

Large groups of mussels can plug water pipes at reservoir pumping stations, water treatment plants, electric generating plants, and factories. Plant managers often use the chemical chlorine, hot-water treatments, and hard work to get rid of the mussels and some-

In Lake Erie, zebra mussels have made thick carpets. In some places there are from thirty thousand to seventy thousand mussels per square yard. When they die, rotting mussels litter beaches, causing bathers to go elsewhere. (M. Parsons, Michigan Sea Grant)

When they grow on the hulls of barges, zebra mussels slow down ships and cause them to use more fuel. This extra load adds to the cost of transporting cargo. (Great Lakes Exotic Species Graphic Library)

times have to shut down plants to clean clogged pipes and machinery. Zebra mussels can plug locks and dams, litter beaches, and stick to boats. They can even grow inside boat motors. Zebra mussels threaten fish and other water animals when they cover the gravelly lake and stream bottoms where some fish lay their eggs.

Zebra mussels also attach to other animals, like clams and crayfish. As the zebra mussels grow, they can kill these animals by blocking important body parts, such as the claws or siphon. (Ontario Ministry of Natural Resources)

Zebra mussels have huge appetites for plankton. Every two days one zebra mussel can eat all the plankton from the water that can fit in a two-liter soft drink bottle. Not much plankton is left after such a feast. Other plankton eaters, like native clams and fish, may starve. Zebra mussels also remove oxygen from the water, and when oxygen levels fall too low, fish and other aquatic animals die.

Zebra mussels have a few natural enemies. Though they are too small and poor tasting for humans to eat, gulls and diving ducks, crayfish, freshwater drum, and yellow perch find them tasty. Yet these animals cannot eat enough of them to control the zebra mussel population.

These zebra mussels have attached to a native clam. It is likely that the small but fast-multiplying zebra mussel will replace the native clam in some lakes and streams. (Chet Childs, Underwater Archaeological Society)

Much about the zebra mussel is still a mystery. Some biologists are trying to raise the mussels in laboratories, but young mussels die before they mature. Something about life in the lab is different from life outdoors, so scientists must study zebra mussels in lakes and streams. They test chemicals to see if they will kill zebra mussels without harming other animals and plants or polluting people's drinking water. At factories, special pumps add chlorine to water taken from lakes or rivers before it is used. Elsewhere people use fast-running water, electric shocks, and special paints to stop the mussels from attaching to hard surfaces.

Many oceangoing ships are now changing ballast water at sea. They blow out the water in the ballast tanks and refill the tanks with seawater. The mussels and other freshwater creatures escape and

How You Can Help

1. Do not take water from an area where zebra mussels have been found. Drain water from bait buckets, the engine compartments of boats, and boat trailers.

2. After you remove a boat from the water, wash its engine, hull, and trailer with chlorine bleach and water. Bleach kills zebra mussels—and everything else in the water—so it must not be used in lakes and rivers.

3. Wash water toys and scuba-diving equipment in chlorine bleach solution.

4. Throw any zebra mussels into the trash—not back in the water.

5. If you find a zebra mussel in a new area, save it. Put it in a jar of rubbing alcohol and give it to a local natural resource manager. Look under "Department of Natural Resources" in the state government listings of your telephone book.

6. For more information on zebra mussels, contact the Zebra Mussel Clearinghouse, New York Sea Grant Extension, 250 Hartwell Hall, SUNY College at Brockport, Brockport, NY 14420.

usually die in the salty ocean. With this method, perhaps fewer exotic species will arrive at ports worldwide. Still, biologists believe that zebra mussels are here to stay. They estimate that by the year 2000, two out of three lakes and rivers in the United States could become a home to these immigrants. We may just have to get used to our new neighbors.

Boaters can help slow the spread of zebra mussels by cleaning any mussels from their boats before launching them in uninfested waters. (Ontario Ministry of Natural Resources)

Getting the word out is an important part of the fight against zebra mussels. (Ontario Ministry of Natural Resources)

Starlings flock in large numbers. In flight their triangular wings make them look like miniature jet fighters. (James R. Page)

The male and female starling look alike. When seen in the right light, their feathers shine with green and purple. During the winter the starling's feathers are speckled with tiny, starlike white patches, for which it likely earned its name. (Dan Schneider)

On October 4, 1960, at Logan International Airport in Boston, Massachusetts, a jet rumbled along the airstrip and rose into the air. A half minute later, the jet struck a flock of more than ten thousand starlings. The plane veered sharply to its left—its engines plugged with dead birds—and plunged into the icy waters of Boston Harbor. Sixty-one of the seventy-two people aboard died in the crash.

Though airplanes often hit a bird or two, a tragedy like this one is rare. More often starlings grab the spotlight for

Bird Gangs: European Starlings

other reasons: eating crops, waking sleepers with their calls, or soiling buildings and streets with their droppings. After starlings roosted for years on the capitol building in Springfield, Illinois, municipal workers cleared no less than eleven tons of droppings from the roof.

Starlings haven't always had such a bad reputation. In the late 1800s, homesick immigrants in many U.S. cities formed clubs to import plants and birds from their homelands.

Starlings seem to nest almost anywhere, in chimneys, mailboxes, and gutters. They have even been found in electrical boxes. (Dan Schneider)

The American Acclimatization Society released some sixty European starlings in Central Park in New York City.

These European starlings, called *Sturnus vulgaris* by scientists, were hardy pioneers. In less than one hundred years, the birds had spread from the East Coast to California and from Canada to Mexico. They made themselves at home on farms, in wooded areas, cities and towns, garbage dumps, and even the parking lots of fast-food restaurants. Ornithologists, scientists who study birds, estimate that today more than 200 million European starlings live in North America. That adds up to three starlings for every house cat in the United States.

The Menu

bees   grapes
beetles   grasshoppers
berries   millipedes
butterflies   moths
crickets   salamanders
earthworms seedlings
garbage

Early in the spring, starlings mate and build nests in cavities in trees, on ledges, or in other sheltered spots. European starlings cannot peck their own nesting holes in trees, so they look for empty holes made by other birds. Sometimes they even chase other birds from their nests and then take over the cavity. The female starling lays a clutch of from four to six pale blue eggs. After twelve days, chicks with huge appetites hatch. Both parent birds spend hours bringing food to their young.

Starlings are hardier than many American birds and very adaptable. In some places, other birds move out when starlings move in. The eastern bluebird and species of small woodpeckers lose the battle for nest sites and food. Starlings are so good at finding food that they leave little for other birds. Starlings often feed together. In a line, they work their way across a field, like police officers looking for a clue.

Ever-hungry starling chicks keep their parents on the fly. In one breeding season, a single pair of starlings may raise two broods of chicks—as many as a dozen young—though some chicks are killed by predators. (Dan Schneider)

Starlings gather an extraordinary amount of food for their young. A bird-watcher once counted three hundred feeding visits made in one day by a pair of starling parents. (James R. Page)

Farmers despise starlings because the birds strip the fruit from strawberry plants, berry bushes, grapevines, and cherry trees. They eat grain from cattle and swine feed troughs and pull up young winter wheat plants to eat the half-sprouted seeds. Starlings can also carry diseases that can sicken hogs and sometimes people.

During the fall and winter, hundreds of thousands of European starlings gather to roost, most often in agricultural areas. So many starlings can wake even the soundest sleeper with their calls. Starlings squeak, whistle, click, and cluck, and the nitrogen in their droppings sometimes kills the trees and plants around the roost.

Such large flocks of starlings often wear out their welcome, and people have tried many ways to scare away these fearless birds. They have put up scarecrows and designed special noise-makers and even have tried playing recordings of starling distress calls. But the birds just fly from one place to another and back. Starlings even seem to like noisy places best because the noise is like a dinner bell—it often means good food.

Farmers kill starlings using guns or chemicals and blow up the birds' roosts with dynamite, while cherry growers have covered their orchards with nets or used pesticides to make starlings sick.

Darting in waves at speeds up to fifty-five miles per hour, large flocks of starlings fascinate observers. How they can fly in such large groups without accident is still a mystery. (James R. Page)

How You Can Help

1. Feed the birds that compete with starlings for food. Many birds like small black-oil sunflower seeds. A feeding platform surrounded by a wire mesh with squares measuring one and one-eighth inch (three centimeters) will keep out starlings while letting smaller birds feed.

2. Or put a tray of food out in the early morning and take it in at noon. Starlings are late feeders—not early birds.

3. Some birds, like woodpeckers, will eat suet, or animal fat. Woodpeckers often feed while perching upside down. Starlings like suet but cannot perch upside down. Hang a suet feeder so the birds must perch upside down to eat.

4. Cover strawberry plants, berry bushes, grapevines, and cherry trees with antibird nets available from garden supply catalogs.

5. Put a wire mesh screen over the chimney opening to keep starlings from nesting in the chimney. Starlings sometimes fall down chimneys when they perch there to warm their feet!

6. Hang a birdhouse for other cavity nesters who fight with starlings for nest sites. Make sure the entrance hole of the birdhouse is no bigger than one and one-half inches (three and four-fifths centimeters) in diameter so that starlings cannot squeeze into it.

7. For more on birds and bird-watching, contact the National Audubon Society, P.O. Box 52529, Boulder, CO 80322.

European Starling Range Map

In several cities, people have sprayed starlings with soapy water during the cold months. Bird feathers are coated with oil, which keeps out moisture and helps the birds stay warm. When the soap washes away the oil, the birds become damp and freeze to death. Whereas some people are happy to get rid of the starlings, others do not like the idea of killing birds by the thousands.

Scarecrows and noisemakers do not foil persistent starlings. (Rob Cardillo)

Though starlings cause trouble, they can help too. They eat large numbers of insects—like Japanese beetles, cutworm moths, and clover weevils—that harm farmers' crops. And some people like starlings so much that they keep them as pets.

Since 1966, the number of European starlings has fallen. Yet clearly, they are here to stay—whether as friend or foe. Some ornithologists suggest that we should now consider them U.S. citizens, not exotic invaders.

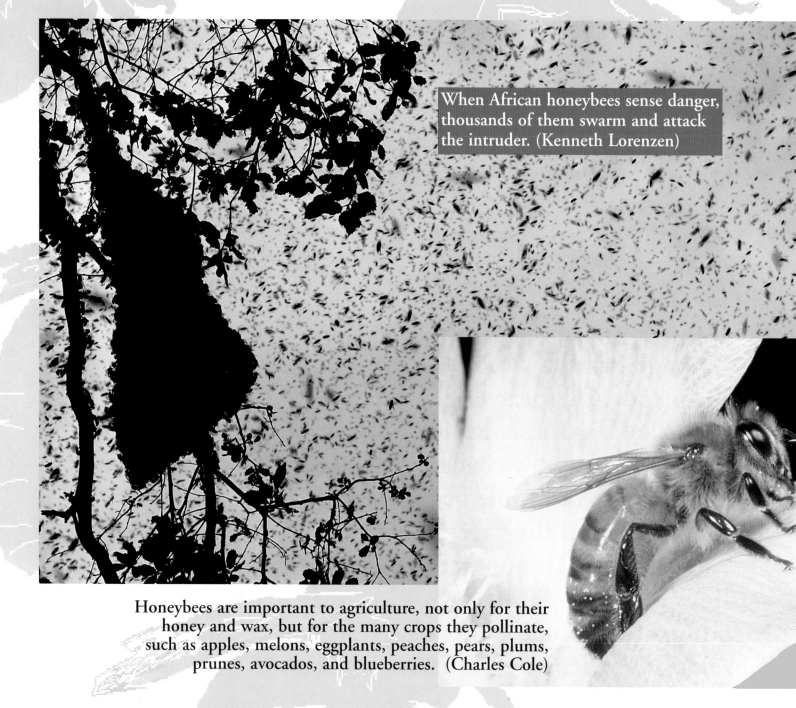

When African honeybees sense danger, thousands of them swarm and attack the intruder. (Kenneth Lorenzen)

Honeybees are important to agriculture, not only for their honey and wax, but for the many crops they pollinate, such as apples, melons, eggplants, peaches, pears, plums, prunes, avocados, and blueberries. (Charles Cole)

J. C. Johnson didn't know what hit him on September 3, 1994. He writhed around on the ground of his yard in Georgetown, Texas, as hundreds of bees swarmed into his ears, nose, and mouth. In three minutes he suffered one thousand stings. The vibrations of Johnson's lawn mower had alarmed a swarm of African honeybees that were living in the walls of a nearby auto repair shop.

Firefighters called to the scene sprayed the bees with fire retardant, while paramedics rushed Johnson to the hospital. On the way, thousands of bees swarmed the ambulance, forcing it to pull over. Bees kept emerging from Johnson's clothing, which paramedics threw from the ambulance, leaving a trail along the hospital route.

Killer Bees: African Honeybees

Three hundred years ago no honeybees lived in North America. European settlers who missed honey as a sweetener had to import them. Beekeepers have long liked European bees because they are easy to handle and make lots of honey.

European honeybees prefer cool climates, however, so when, in the 1950s, Brazilian government officials wanted to boost honey making in their own country, they needed to find honeybees that could tolerate the blazing hot Brazilian weather. Professor Warwick Kerr imported

from Africa several dozen queens of *Apis mellifera scutellata,* known as the African honeybee. (*Apis* means "bee," and *mellifera* means "honey carrier.") When the queens accidentally escaped, they formed colonies in the wild. From Brazil, the African bees spread northward.

African bees soon got the nickname "killer bees" because they are more nervous than their European counterparts and will readily fight to defend their hive against an attacker. Swarms of African bees attacked and killed farm animals that could not run away or hide. After swarms killed several people, the "killer bees" made headlines, and they have been in the news ever since. On October 15, 1990, researchers found the first colony of African honeybees to arrive on their own in the United States—in Hidalgo, Texas.

Some people imagine swarms of "killer bees" searching for people to attack. This could be the plot of a horror movie, but it is not really what happens. Like many creatures, honeybees protect their homes from predators. Each bee has only one stinger, armed with venom. When a bee stings an intruder, it leaves its stinger and part of its body in its victim and then dies.

Honeybees live in colonies made up of one queen bee, thousands of worker bees, and hundreds of drones. This African queen has been tagged by researchers. (Scott Camazine)

Both African and European honeybees have light brown-and-black–striped bodies, translucent wings, and bulging black eyes. In fact, the two kinds of bees look so much alike that even scientists have trouble telling them apart just by looking at them.

Scientists disagree about how

African honeybees build hives in a variety of places—in trees or hedgerows, under cliff ledges, or in enclosed spaces, such as buildings. (Kenneth Lorenzen)

dangerous the African bees are and how much trouble they may cause in North America. In the United States each year, fifty people die from bee stings. Some are allergic to bee venom

and can die from a single sting. Others die because they have been stung so many times. Even as few as ten stings can cause a medical emergency in someone who is not allergic. Though attacks by swarms are rare—about as likely as getting hit by lightning—this may soon change. Since May 1991, African bees have stung more than two hundred people in the United States, and in July 1993 they killed their first U.S. citizen.

How You Can Help

1. If you find a bee colony, do not disturb it. Report wild colonies or swarms of bees to a natural resource manager or pest control agency. Look under your local government or U.S. government heading in your telephone directory.

2. Fill in possible nesting sites, such as holes in trees or outside walls near your home. Put screens on the top of waterspouts. Clean up piles of brush or junk. African bees have made nests in old tires, rusting cars, and snarls of branches.

3. When you see bees foraging for pollen and nectar, do not bother them. Move slowly. Bees do not like fast movements. Killing a bee makes it release a scent that calls other bees to fend off danger.

4. If you are allergic to bee stings, carry a special doctor-prescribed bee sting kit with you. You may want to ask an allergy specialist if desensitization is right for you.

5. If you are attacked by bees, run away as fast as you can. Bees are slow fliers. Break the bees' line of sight by zigzagging through trees or brush. Get indoors, if possible.

6. If you are stung many times, get medical help right away.

7. Wear light-colored clothes when outdoors. Bees are less attracted to light colors. Avoid picnics.

8. For more information, contact the United States Department of Agriculture, Extension Service, Information Staff, Room 3333, South Building, Washington, DC 20250.

For more than twenty years, entomologists in North and South America have been studying and tracking the African honeybees. Though entomologists cannot stop the bees from coming to the United States, they can warn people about them. They recommend using chemical pesticides (such as wasp killers), carbon dioxide, or dry chemical fire extinguishers to kill nuisance bees. These methods work well if the bees are inside a cavity, such as a hole in a tree. But if the bees are in a cluster on a tree branch, they may fly off in a swarm while being sprayed. Then they may sting nearby people or animals. Researchers have also tried spraying bees with a mixture of liquid dish soap and water. Bees cannot fly out of a cluster if their wings are wet, and detergent kills the bees by clogging their lungs.

Some entomologists believe that African bees will stay in the warm southern states. Others think that they will survive in all but the coldest parts of the country, such as the northern Midwest. Yet entomologists have no doubt that African bees are in North America to stay. We will have to learn to live peacefully with them. To do this, we need to understand the bees and take care.

Beekeepers use smoke to calm African honeybees. (Scott Camazine)

Traveling beekeepers transport hives of honeybees from orchard to orchard. Scientists fear that African bees will be unsafe for pollinating crops, such as the almond trees shown here, because they cannot be handled safely by beekeepers. (Kenneth Lorenzen)

Further Reading

Boyle, Robert H. "In Shock Over Shells." *Sports Illustrated,* October 15, 1990, pp. 88–95.

Corbo, Margaret Sigl, and Diane Marr Barras. *Arnie, the Darling Starling.* Boston: Houghton Mifflin, 1983.

Facklam, Howard, and Margery Facklam. *Insects.* New York: Twentieth-Century Press, 1994.

———. *Parasites.* New York: Twentieth-Century Press, 1994.

"Killer Bees Approach." *Current Events,* August 30–September 3, 1993, p. 13.

Labonte, Gail. *Leeches, Lampreys, and Other Cold-blooded Bloodsuckers.* New York: Watts, 1991.

Lampton, Christopher. *Insect Attack.* Brookfield, Conn.: Millbrook Press, 1992.

Miller, C. "There's No Stopping Those Starlings!" *Ranger Rick,* December 1993, pp. 16–21.

Peissel, Michael, and Missy Allen. *Dangerous Insects.* New York: Chelsea House, 1993.

Pringle, Laurence. *Killer Bees.* New York: Morrow Junior Books, 1990.

Westrup, H. "Killer Bees Spreading in U.S." *Current Science,* December 16, 1994, pp. 8–9.

Index